What's

featuring Auntie P

Sharing?

by Patricia Kearney

Illustrations by Dexter Santos

"Unity is strength... when there is teamwork and collaboration, wonderful things can be achieved."

MATTIE STEPANEK (1990–2004), AMERICAN TEENAGE POET

"Our duty, as men and women, is to proceed as if limits to our ability did not exist. We are collaborators in creation."

PIERRE TEILHARD DE CHARDIN (1881-1955)
FRENCH JESUIT THEOLOGIAN AND SCIENTIST

DEDICATION

I dedicate this book to those who believe that the spirit of sharing can be a source of positive energy for the whole community. This story is about sharing and teamwork. Hopefully, children of all ages will be inspired by the garden project and take joy in sharing new experiences together. Pass it on!

Connolly, Hayes & Heffernan Publishers
P. O. Box 40322
Pittsburgh, PA 15201
www.auntiep.com

Editor: Sydnee Bagovich

What's Sharing? First Edition May 4, 2013
ISBN 978-0-615-62506-5 (Library of Congress)

Cataloging-in-Publication Data
Library of Congress Control Number: 2012910250

What's Sharing? \Kearney-McCarty, Patricia

The paper used in this publication meets the minimum requirements of the American National Standards for Information Sciences—Permanence of Paper for the Printed Library Materials ANSI Z39.48-1992.

Special Thanks: Petra Kearney Lopez, David (Little D) Lopez, Leah Lopez, David Lopez Sr., Soo Clark, Carolann Cioffi DeSantis, Joe Conwell, Deepak Ghosh, Frank Andrews, Paul Cosentino and The Boilermaker Jazz Band (www.boilermakerjazzband.com) and Ernst (www.mccartyart.com)

Illustrations: Dexter Santos
Design: Paulette Green, P Green Design
Photo back cover: Michele D'Emo

Auntie P has just hopped off the train.

She can't wait to see her niece and nephew, Petra and Little D. After sitting the whole time during the train ride, Auntie P decides to walk a few blocks. She sees them! There they are! "Hi, Auntie P," the children yell. They run to greet her, giving her kisses and hugs as if she had been away forever! Petra and Little D love calling their Aunt Patricia *Auntie P.* It makes them both giggle inside.

As soon as Auntie P gets settled in, the whole family decides to sit outside and have a nice glass of lemonade. It's a lovely day today.

"Oh, delicious lemonade," exclaims Auntie P. "It really hits the spot!" Petra's Auntie P usually visits Petra's family in February, around her birthday. She always travels by train and carries one piece of luggage. Petra and her brother, Little D, look forward to Auntie P's visits, knowing that she will tell them about her recent travels and about her love of music from the 1920s, 1930s and 1940s. This time Auntie P plans to spend a few months with the family.

Everyone is waiting for Auntie P to recount her adventures of the last few months. Petra's mother, Leah, asks Auntie P, "How was your last trip? Did you enjoy your weekend in Maryland?" "Ah, at Glen Echo Park!" says Auntie P. "What a delight."

"Oh, my goodness," says Auntie P, "Glen Echo Park in Maryland is one of the most wonderful places. In the early days, Glen Echo Park was the premier amusement park serving the area until 1968. They had a carousel, tea cup ride and bumper car ride!

Now the park is used for cultural organizations, art classes, dancing, concerts, and the carousel has been restored!" "Can we ride on it?" asks Little D. "Yes you can!" exclaims Auntie P. "Kids and grownups—everyone! Isn't that wonderful?"

Reflecting on her visit to Glen Echo Park, Auntie P continues her story. "I headed straight for the Spanish Ballroom. The reason for being there was to hear my favorite swing band and dance, dance, dance," said Auntie P. "The ballroom was built in 1933, I believe." "Gee, Auntie P," said Petra, "that's really a long time ago." "That's true, Petra," laughs Auntie P. "I wish I had lived during that time." "Oh, I don't think so, Auntie P," said Petra, "then maybe we wouldn't get to see you!"

"The great thing about these swing dances," Auntie P explains, "is that everyone gets to dance the night away. No one is left out. Dancers get to change partners and try different dance styles. It's a great event always."

"We have some news to tell you, Auntie P," says Petra's mother. "Go ahead, Petra, tell Auntie P your good news." "Oh, Auntie P," said Petra, hardly able to contain herself, "I've been chosen to head a project for my class at school! Everyone in my class will be involved in growing a garden, and I'm the project manager. Isn't that great?"

"Oh, that's wonderful, Petra," said Auntie P. "Congratulations on being chosen. What a great experience for you and your class."

BLUEBERRIES!

"Isn't every class level going to be involved?" asks Petra's father, David. "Oh, no," replies Petra. "It's just going to be my own class. It's probably easier and simpler. It will only be ours to share."

"I decided that it will be a blueberry patch. I love blueberries," Petra tells everyone. "Oh, I just love them, too," says Petra's mother, Leah. "They are great with cereal in the morning."

"I'd really like to try to grow something, too,"
says Little D. "I'd be really happy to grow tomatoes."
"No, it's much easier, Little D, if everything is the
same. It's my class, and it's going to be all blueberries.
A nice blueberry patch," explains Petra.

"Petra," asks Auntie P, "Little D seems sad that he can't have fun with the project, too. Is there some way you might include him? You know, energetic teamwork can be helpful in accomplishing your goals in any project," says Auntie P.

"I'm the project manager," replies Petra. "It's all my idea, but Little D can do some work if he wants." "That's not really what I mean, Petra," remarks Auntie P. "Maybe you can figure out a way to let him have fun and share in planning the garden as well. You'll eventually get bored with blueberries, blueberries, blueberries."

The next day Petra's school mate, Clooney, stops by. His parents, Rosie and Margaret, are dropping him off at Petra's house. They are on their way to an exercise class. "Good morning," yells Clooney. "Nice to see you all. Hi Auntie P! See you later," he calls to his parents. "They're on their way to an exercise dance class that begins with a Z," Clooney tells Petra.

Immediately Clooney and Petra start to talk about the class project. They are so excited about getting a plot of ground ready for the project of planting. Clooney confides in Petra that news about a garden is being passed around the school and that some of the younger kids on his block would like to plant something, too.

Clooney tells Petra that he has his heart set on working on the gardening project and is excited about planting kirbies. "Why does everyone want something different instead of wonderful blueberries?" asks Petra. "You can make pancakes, you can have them in your yogurt, you can make a blueberry pie and you can make a smoothie. You can't make a delicious pie or smoothie with kirbies," says Petra.

"Petra," says Clooney, "I really have my heart set on planting what I want, and that would be kirbies. They may be small, but they are very tasty," says Clooney, "and they don't have seeds. That's very important sometimes, you know."

After some discussion, Petra realizes that Clooney is right. "Yes, it is right that everyone should have the chance to plant what they would like to plant," remarks Petra. "I guess I will have to change my plan on sharing this project."

While walking farther down the block, Petra and Clooney see Murray. Murray runs up to Petra and Clooney and tells them that he heard about the garden and that he wants to plant soup.

"Soup? You don't plant soup, Murray," exclaims Petra. "You buy that in the supermarket, in cans or in a pouch. There's no such fruit or vegetable as soup, Murray," says Petra. "Gee," exclaims Murray, "I love soup. My Tante Ruchel and Tante Libba make it for me all the time. No soup?" Petra and Clooney realize that they don't know what to do about Murray. They say good-bye to Murray and tell him that they will see him tomorrow. "Get home safe, Murray. Make sure your mother knows where you are. Go right home," says Clooney.

Petra tells Auntie P and Little D about her conversation with Clooney and that she has decided to have everyone in the neighborhood join in planning and planting in the garden. Little D and Auntie P are thrilled that the garden project is now going to be a project shared by everyone. Petra tells Little D and Auntie P that she and Clooney saw Murray on the block yesterday. "Murray said that he wanted to grow *soup*, Auntie P. I don't know what to do about this. I guess he's just too young to be part of the project."

Auntie P offers some words to Petra. "Perhaps you and your classmates should ask Murray what kind of soup he likes. Maybe that would help."

The next day Petra, Clooney and Little D see Murray in front of his house, and Petra remembers to ask him, "What kind of soup do you like, Murray?" "One of my favorite soups is carrots and ginger," Murray tells everyone with a broad smile. "That's it then, **carrots**," they all shout! "Murray can grow the **carrots**!"

"I really wanted to grow soup," says Murray, "but I can grow carrots." Petra is a little worried about Murray. Little D tells Petra, "Don't worry about Murray. We will just teach him all about making soup and growing the ingredients. After all, he's only four!" "We'll all have fun together, that's for sure," says Clooney.

"We need to find a plot for our garden, Petra," says Clooney. "That's the most important thing. Let's keep looking on the block for a nice garden area." All of a sudden they see Deepak coming down the block. "Hello, hey!" Deepak greets everyone.

HERBS!

"Hi, everyone! What a nice day," says Deepak. "I've heard about the garden project, and I'm so excited. I was hoping that you will let me set out a little plot and grow all of the herbs!" Deepak, who is in the third grade, has learned a lot about herbs from his father and mother. "My father, Raj, and my mother, Pallavi, as you may know, have a restaurant. They said they were so excited about the class garden project. They want to offer us a plot of land on the same block as the restaurant! It's a huge plot! We can plant even more vegetables. Isn't that wonderful news?"

This news creates great excitement for Petra and Clooney especially. Clooney says, "Everything seems to be falling into place about this project, Petra. We now even have the garden plot!"

It seems as if everyone in the neighborhood has now heard about the garden project. Neighbors Jeremy and Kim come to greet everyone. "Hi Petra and Clooney! Auntie P, it's so good to see you," says Jeremy. "Kim and I are home from the army and we'd love to help out the kids. We need something to do! We can plot out the measurements, put up trellises and sticks for the peppers and tomatoes, and even put in a rain barrel or two." "We'd love to help out!" says Kim.

"That will be so wonderful," says Clooney. "We can have everyone in the whole neighborhood involved! We'll have a community garden!"

Everyone is excited about the garden and is working so hard to make sure that everything is done. Little D and his friend, Maria, tell Auntie P about all of the plants that everyone is putting in the ground to make up the community garden. "Sharing is turning out to be fun, Auntie P," says Little D. "Potatoes, tomatoes, lettuce, Clooney's kirbies, beans, peas, Maria's mushrooms, squash, onions, beets, Murray's carrots and ginger, Petra's blueberries, my strawberries and Deepak's herbs—cilantro, mint, basil, parsley, dill, rosemary, sage, oregano, chives—oh, I can't wait."

"Now, all we have to do is wait," Petra tells everyone. "We have to wait and wait patiently for the plants to grow, and we will see a beautiful community garden!" "It's going to be the best project in the neighborhood ever," exclaims Clooney. "Yes, wait, wait and wait patiently for everything to grow," says Little D. "I hope I can do it. Wait, wait and *wait*. Do you think it will rain?"

Today is a special day. All of the children are standing by the windows at Deepak's house watching the rain come down outside. "Even though we can't go outside," says Deepak, "the rain is bringing the right amount of water for our garden each day. I just know it." "It's the only time I love the rain!" says Petra with a huge grin. "All of us agree with that, Petra," replies Clooney. "We may not be able to play outside this spring, but we do need this wonderful rain for our garden to grow."

"I think I see things growing already," says Little D. "I really do!"

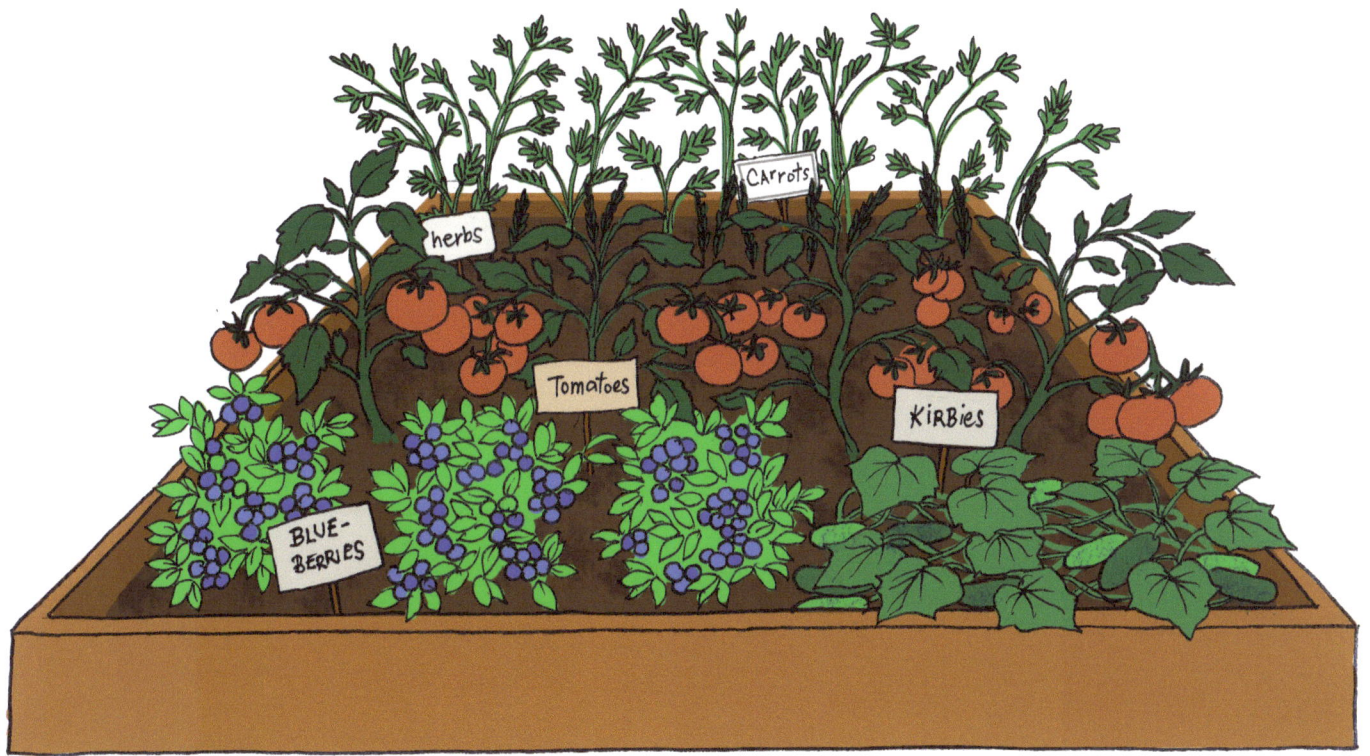

Then one day it happened. It stopped raining and the sun was out all day. The children decided to run to the garden plot so that they could see what was happening. A number of months had now passed. Standing at the garden plot, what do you think they saw? After all of their waiting and waiting, the garden had bloomed. The plants had become large and green. They saw so many different types of vegetables and fruits that appeared like magic all over the garden plot.

There it was before them—a beautiful community garden. Everyone seemed to come outside to see the garden at the same time. "We grew so many different things, and they all work together in the garden," exclaims Petra. "My fabulous blueberries, the tomatoes, potatoes, peas, green beans, parsley, lettuce, squash, Deepak's herbs—rosemary, sage, oregano, chives, dill." "My kirbies," reminds Clooney. "And don't forget Murray's soup," pipes up Little D.

"Oh, yes," says Murray grinning from ear to ear, "my carrots and ginger, for a really good soup! Thank you everyone for including me and teaching me how to grow things," says Murray. "What did you grow, Maria?" asks Murray. "Mushrooms, three different kinds," replies Maria. "Oh, they would make a really good soup," exclaims Murray.

"We found out what sharing really is, didn't we, Auntie P?" asks Petra. "Yes," says Little D. "It's not just about sharing our toys, is it, Auntie P? Do we have to share, Auntie P?" "No, Little D, it's really up to you," said Auntie P. "You don't have to share, but look at the joy it gave to everyone. You all shared in planning the garden. You shared in the physical work, and you shared your knowledge by teaching the younger children how to plant.

By sharing, you brought out a positive spirit in the whole community. Everyone wanted to help. You are a great project manager, Petra.

You've turned the neighborhood into **One Big Salad**," said Auntie P.

"Oh, no, I feel one of Auntie P's dances coming on," whispers Petra to Clooney with **A Big Salad** smile on her face.

"Well, kids," exclaims Auntie P, "in honor of Murray's carrots, I think we should all get up and learn the *Bunny Hop*! What else could it be?"

"Oh, the Bunny Hop is so yesterday," says Petra. "Only you would make us hop, hop, hop."

"Who cares? It will get **everyone** up. Let's move and start hopping! It's better to get up and move than to sit and watch your life go by," says Auntie P. "Learning the Bunny Hop is simple dimple, kids! I've got my dancing shoes on. Here we go! Everyone, let's share some Bunny Hop!"

Da, da, da, da, da, da! Da, da, da, da, da, da! Da, da, da, da, da, da! HOP! HOP! HOP! Da, da, da, da, da, Da, da, da, da, da, da! Da, da, da, da, da, da! HOP! HOP! HOP!

Notes to Teachers

It would be simple dimple to show the kids
in your class how to do the Bunny Hop dance.
Some reference videos are below.
Have fun!

The Bunny Hop videos

http://www.youtube.com/watch?v=VCTWSySXnOY&feature=related
http://www.youtube.com/watch?v=m23NrmJwlEY

Glen Echo Park Partnership for Arts and Culture

http://www.glenechopark.org/

artist
Dexter Santos

Dexter Santos has been drawing ever since he was 3 years old. His fascination with art started with the comic books he read and collected as well as the children's books that stimulated his imagination as a kid.

All throughout his elementary and high school years, Dexter participated in any event that had anything to do with drawing or painting and won for himself a handful of awards.

Continuing his passion for art as an adult, Dexter has seen his artwork manifested in art shows, on postcards, t-shirts, the Internet, the back of a bus, and even projected on a movie theater screen. This is the first time Dexter has illustrated for a children's book and he is excited and honored to tell the story of Auntie P and the wonderful lessons she imparts to young children.

Dexter has a BFA in Character Animation and Visual Effects from the Academy of Art University in San Francisco and currently resides in Santa Clara, California. Aside from being an artist, Dexter is also a nationally renowned blues dance teacher and dancer. In his spare time, he likes to social dance, sing, play his ukulele, and go on afternoon motorcycle rides.

Find out more about Dexter's artwork at **dexterityink.com** and his dancing at **dextersantos.com.**

.

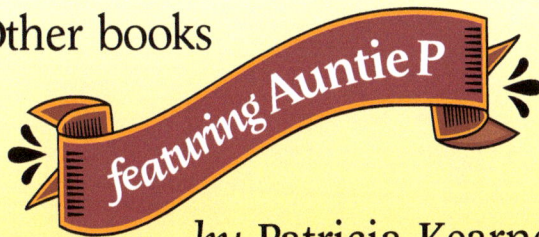

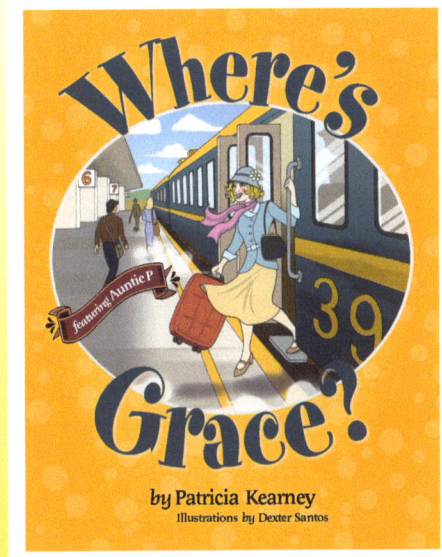